YOUR PROBLEM IS THAT YOU'RE MULTITALENTED

DR SAMUEL EKUNDAYO

DEDICATION

To all the multi-talented and multi-gifted kings and queens of this generation and the ones to come.

To my amazing Dudushewa and Treasure, my one and only wife, Dr Blessing Ekundayo, my wonderful children, Oluwasemiloore, and Oluwaferanmi Ekundayo who allowed me to use my gifts as an author to bless my generation. Thank you for your love and sacrifice. I couldn't have written this book without your support. I am incredibly indebted to you.

To my parents, Dr John and Pastor Mary Ekundayo, my parents in-love, Rev (Dr) Ezekiel and Rev (Prof) Esther Agbaje, and my amazing siblings, Gloria Olajesu, and Grace Boluwatife, thank you for your constant support. I am very grateful.

To my amazing team; from my book cover designer, Mila, to my editor and friend, Pastor Sam Adetiran, my graphics designer and mentee, Opeoluwa Adebakin, my phenomenal Executive Assistant, Ifeoluwa Arowosegbe, and my amazing mentee Dr Adediwura Arowosegbe. Thank you all for your amazing inputs into making this book a success. I could not have done it without you. I am very grateful. I pray that you all would maximise your potential in life in Jesus' name.

To my friend and sister, Debola Deji-Kurunmi (DDK), who God used to spur me on when the vision of this book was almost left on the back burner. Thank you so much for encouraging me to pick it up and write it. I honour and celebrate you.

ACKNOWLEDGEMENTS

Creating this book has been a personal journey of discovery in the course of which I have learnt and met several people who have mentored, coached, and counselled me along the way. I cannot but acknowledge that my achievements in life are the total of all the people, experiences, and learnings that God has brought my way. This book is evidence of that reality in my life.

I would like to appreciate my wife, Dr Blessing Ekundayo. Thank you for always pushing me to be my best. You always encourage me to push out all of God's deposits within me and I could not have asked God for a better wife, even if I tried. You are the best wife in the entire universe and I am grateful for you. I love you so much.

I want to thank my parents in the Lord, Pastor David and Dr Adesayo Adelowo, who constantly give me the room to spread my wings and fly. Leaders like you are rare in our world. God bless you.

I am grateful to my mentors, Bishop Bob Alonge and Mummy Adeteju Alonge, for their constant encouragement and support in birthing every idea God has given me. Thank you for always being there for me. I am so grateful for your roles in my life.

In the course of writing this book, I have drawn on the stories of many great men and women, leaders and influencers that I have learnt from to become who I am today, and to pen the wisdom in this book. May this book give back to you more than you have taught and invested in me.

CONTENTS

INTRODUCTION

Is being multitalented a curse or a blessing?

Is being a jack of all trades, a person with many skills really a blessing? There are many words in the dictionary to define people with multi-talents. Often referred to as, multi-skilled, well-rounded, versatile, and adaptable, one can think of this person as someone a lot of people would envy. To be frank, people envy such people and admire them. For instance, at school, they're often well-rounded in most of the subjects, as a polymath, they brilliantly scale many courses. These are usually the people we call 'Smart' in school because of their well-roundedness in most subjects. Remember that guy or girl in your class that appeared to know almost everything? They are usually at the top of the class in almost every subject. I was one of those, not necessarily the smartest of the bunch but I was well-rounded. While I didn't exactly see it that way back in my primary or high school days, it was clear I had many interests.

The dictionary defines a multitalented person as someone 'having more than one special talent or skill'[1]. This definition stands out to me because it really defines me. I wrote this book because I struggled for most of my life with my many talents. It got me so busy but not effective. While I was a centre of attraction or attention most of the time, I found that I was not effective and productive. I was not known for anything in particular. This is the danger of being a multi talented human being.

If you do not know what to do with your many skills and gifts, you would come to a point in your life where you will feel you're wasting away, and this comes with a lot of frustration. I

---

1   Merriam Webster Dictionary - https://www.merriam-webster.com/dictionary/multitalented

can imagine you wondering 'but how'? especially if you haven't quite felt the frustration of being multi-talented. Some people, including you, reading this may not yet have come to that point of frustration and you probably are at the point where you are still enjoying the attention and attraction it brings. You are in this territory of pride; enjoying being the cynosure of all eyes and what appears as though everyone needs you or wants you to do one or two things for them. I can assure you though, it is only a matter of time before you start realising those people calling for you are just using you and are not really seeing you as a person of value because you are yet to define your value.

One of my objectives with writing this book is to help you navigate your many gifts and skills towards becoming a person of value. Of what use is being multiskilled, multitalented, and versatile without becoming a person of value and influence? If you do not become a person of value despite your many gifts, then they will become a curse for you, but if you can become a person of value and influence, you will enjoy having them and the blessings that come along.

In the remaining pages of this book, I shared the story of my struggles with being a multitalented and multi-gifted individual. I then proceed to share why if not handled correctly, the many gifts could be a curse and not a blessing. Furthermore, I discussed the seeming value or benefits to let you know why some people do not consider it a problem until it is almost too late or never at all. Of course, I also shared what I have come to learn as the solution to the frustration of the multi-talented individual based on my experience and what has led to my effectiveness and upshot of value. I then show you the value of adopting this solution to your own life. I concluded with the inspiring stories of a few other people relaying the same solution in their lives and their journey to show you why you too must imbibe the solution for your effectiveness, value, and influence in life. Follow me on this journey of realisation, discovery, clarity, and mindset change.

Without a doubt, this book will cause a shift in your mindset about how you view yourself, your talents, and your gifts. It will also help you value yourself a lot more than you have ever done and help you realise the true blessings in all your endowments. I can assure you God does not waste resources. This means He has a purpose for every single gift and talent He gave you. It is your responsibility to discover that purpose, channel those gifts rightly to fulfil it, and become the person of value and influence you were created to be. This is very important because we are going to give an account of every gift and talent we've been given. God will surely ask you what you have done with those gifts. You need to be productive and effective with them so that you are not referred to as an "unprofitable servant"[2]

It is not going to be an easy journey because it is a sacrificial one. I can tell you this from experience. You will miss the attention and attraction that your many talents and gifts bring to your life for a season, but if you persevere through that valley between the mountains of frustration and effectiveness, you will come out as fine gold, valuable, productive, and priceless. But if you choose to remain on the mountain of frustration where being the cynosure of all eyes is what you feed on and has come to be your source of esteem, you will likely die ordinary and never realise the real and full benefits and potential of your gifts and talents.

Let the journey begin.

---

2   Matthew 25:30 (KJV)

Chapter 1

MY STORY

Growing up: my many talents

It was a beautiful day in the city of Ibadan, Nigeria. The sun was at its peak and nothing could go wrong. I was invited to a friend's birthday party outdoors. We were just teenagers, but the party was not exclusive to us. Our parents were also invited. At least, around a hundred people attended the party.

The Master of Ceremony decided it was time to entertain the audience and he asked for one of the teenagers to come and showcase their talent. He was particularly asking for someone who could dance. I put my hand up with so much confidence. Before I knew it, I was on stage, dancing to Sisqo's song – *Got to get it*. If you're my age, you are likely to remember this song vividly. It was one of the reigning songs then. I was breakdancing to it and I got the crowd up in amazement. They cheered and cheered in amusement purely entertained by my prowess. Some of them sprayed me money on the dance floor to encourage me, it was unbelievable. It was the first time in my life I would be sprayed so much money for dancing. I couldn't believe it.

That single event made me believe I was born to be a dancer. In fact, some of the parents in attendance said almost the same thing. And for years, I was excited by this discovery that I could dance and entertain people enough for them to pay me for it. I remember offering to dance in the Teenagers church in the church we attended then. When I got to the University too, I offered to dance several times in church fellowship programs and concerts.

The popular actor

At the university, I joined the drama group of my fellowship and I remember one of the very first playlets we did, I had acted a role that brought out my witty side, and people could not believe it. I made everyone laugh so much, yet they didn't lose the message of the playlet. After that particular event, many people came up to me telling me they thought I was born to act. Their encouragement assured me I was good at it.

Several playlets after that one, I was convinced I had a gift not just for acting but for comedy. Every time I was on stage, people were sure they were going to laugh their heads off, and not only that, they were going to enjoy the show. I became the centre of attraction for most playlets and soon after, other fellowships started inviting me to be a part of their shows and events. Every audition I did, I scaled through. It was clear I had a gift.

The gifted teacher

Another instance was my gift of teaching. Way back in my early days of school, particularly my high school days, I was a favourite amongst my friends for the way I helped explain the very same things the teacher had explained to us in class. I mean, after each class, they would gather around me and it often would seem like I was assisting the teacher in ensuring they got what had been taught. It was very clear my fellow students saw the gift in me.

It became a norm for most of the subjects we took in school then, especially the ones that I enjoyed and was passionate about. I didn't particularly favour some subjects then including Mathematics and Chemistry but most of the others, I had a hang of, I enjoyed teaching my mates. The ability to communicate clearly made the exercise enjoyable. In no time, my mates started to refer to me as 'Prof' or 'Professor'. I nicknamed myself 'Smart' then, a name I coined from my initials. It spelt 'SMAT' if I used the initials of the names given to me by my parents, but I think the pride had started to get into me then, so I had to give myself one of my friend's names just so I could get the 'R' to complete the name 'SMART'. The name was Rotimi. I lied to many that my parents gave me the name just so I would have the 'R' in the initials. Now and then, till my early university days, you would hear my friends yell 'Smart' or 'Prof Smart' from time to time, especially when I started to tell everyone who cared to listen about my dream of becoming a Professor.

Teaching is a gift and it has been a gift since my early school days. Perhaps I should say communication is the true gift. I can communicate quite effectively and clearly to a small group of people or a very large audience. In fact, if it was a topic I am passionate about, for instance, the topic of purpose, I could speak for a whole day without getting tired and needing to eat. I would completely feed on the energy that stems from the passion I have for communicating with people.

God bless teachers like Mrs. Oni.

One of the most profound experiences of my life was during my time in Singapore. My family – my dad, mum, and my three sisters – moved to Singapore in 2006. My dad arrived there the year before. Miraculously, after my bachelor's degree, I secured a Master of Science admission into the prestigious Nanyang Technological University. During my study there, one day I saw an advertisement for an International Toastmasters Speech competition. My passion for speaking and communication would not let me see such an advertisement and walk away. I applied. Some of my friends were trying to discourage me saying no one would hear my accent on a stage like that, but I didn't give in to their words.

Some days after applying I got an email detailing the process of the competition. It was like an 'American idol' style audition. I went in and aced the audition. We were given a topic to speak on impromptu. I can't quite remember the topic I spoke on, but it went down well with the judges and I saw that they all had a smile on their faces. I was convinced they liked me. That fuelled my confidence to keep on going on.

I should mention here that in my high school days, I had been headhunted to join the debating club of the school and we went for several competitions. I was in my 6th year, which should have been my 5th but I repeated a whole year because I failed a major exam in my third year at the school. It was a painful experience, but I had learned from it, so I was doing well at this time. I remember this experience quite vividly – one hot afternoon, one of my teachers, the matron of the literary and debating club stormed into our class and called my name along-side a few other students. We were not sure why, but she asked us to follow her to the staff room.

We got to the staff room and the usual arrangement had changed. It had been set up to sort of have a stage. She asked us to sit down and said, 'Welcome, everyone. I have called you here to give you an opportunity of a lifetime. I want you to pick a paper from the bowl on the table in front of you. In the bowl are some topics you would speak on impromptu. Give it your best shot. Good luck'. I can't quite recollect if I was the first speaker or not, but I remember the moment I opened my mouth to speak, everyone in the room burst into laughter. It was as though I was performing comedy. Some of the teachers laughed so strongly they fell off their chairs. It didn't take long for me to realise what they were laughing about – my accent! See, I hailed from a part of Western Nigeria with a funny accent. People from my state of origin were usually very brilliant but their English accent if unrefined can sound quite alarmingly funny – such was my case. My accent hadn't been refined and no one had taught me how to do that.

The only person who did not laugh in the room was Mrs. Oni – the Matron of the literary and debating club who headhunted me. She wore a stern look and said, 'We need to work on your accent, but you spoke quite confidently'. Some days later, my name was called amongst the recruits of the prestigious club. I could not believe it. The scene of the staff room lingered in my head, but Mrs Oni saw something most people did not see. She saw my gift as an orator and communicator and she would not let my unrefined accent blind her to it. Over the next few weeks, she would work with me for hours and days refining my accent. She explained why I had to communicate clearly because we were headed for some competitions in high places including TV stations and government houses. I had to cooperate with her. I was glad when she one day announced I was ready. I didn't think I was, but she said I was, so I believed her.

The next thing I knew was that we were being groomed for a major competition. It was the competition commissioned by the State Governor at the time which was tagged, *Lam Adesina Interschool Debating Competition*. Our school was shortlisted to participate in the competition. We went for the preliminary rounds and Mrs Oni asked me to lead the group. We won all the preliminary rounds we competed in and got into the finals with one of the best schools in the state – Command Day Secondary School, a military school with a great reputation. We battled them in the finals live on State TV. We did not win but it was a very tight round that almost every judge said there just had to be a winner and it was a tight call for them. In the entire state, our school moved up ranks in one of the best schools based on that year's competition. That was when it became clear to me that I had a gift of communication. Thanks to Mrs Oni who saw the raw gold in me and never gave up. She was determined to put me through the process of refinement, so I could come out as fine gold. We need more teachers like Mrs Oni who would stop at nothing to make sure their pupils come out as fine gold.

The International Toastmasters Champion

I enrolled for the International Toastmasters Competition in Singapore with confidence from my High School days in Nigeria. We went through about 2 or 3 preliminary rounds and I scaled them all. I was one of the 10 contestants to qualify for the finals amongst many others who registered for the competition. The day of the grand finale came. We had been told we would speak on any topic of our choice to inspire the audience.

I walked into the large Lecture Theatre where the event was held that day and I could not believe my eyes. It was filled to the brim. So many expectant people. I could see it on their faces. They were ready for the magic the speakers were going to perform. Simply put, they came ready to be inspired by our speeches. It was the final. There was no more room for mistakes. It was an international competition and the best of the best have made it to this final showdown.

I recall I was neither the first nor the last speaker. I was somewhere in the middle. The first speaker took the stage and the young man dazzled. I remember, he spoke on the topic, 'In Pursuit of Happiness'. Every word, phrase, and sentence appeared to be a satisfying gulp for the audience, like an acceptable offering. I couldn't imagine anyone beating the young man. He was impeccable and grabbed the audience's attention from the beginning to the end. When he was done, there was loud and deafening applause for his awesome speech. I am sure the whole room could go home after that amazing speech but for the promise of nine more excellent speakers waiting for their turn. If I was on the panel of judges, I would have just given it to the young man without hearing anyone else speak. He was so convincing that he sounded like no one else could beat him.

The second speaker stood up. She was a young lady possibly in her early 20s. She had an impeccable command of English that reminded me of my terrible accent some years back. No, she was not bad, she was good! She was amazing! I could listen to her a whole day without flinching. She brought her A-game to the competition and you could see she was gifted. By the time she was done, there was also deafening applause in the room. While it was not my turn yet, I was almost getting discouraged, more like assured I was not going to win. The first two speakers had the audience clapping so loudly. I wondered if I could ever beat them.

My turn came, and I remember speaking on the topic, *Who are you and where are you going*? I spoke about how in life it is important to be clear about two key things in order to live effectively – our identity and destiny. It was a topic I was and still very passionate about. I spoke with so much energy, conviction, and power. You could almost hear a pin drop in the room. No one said a word till I finished. I could tell I had drawn the audience in. I looked at the audience in their eyeballs. I felt the connection. I could tell they were all listening quite intently to every word. By the time I started speaking, I had lost every nerve I got into the room with or the worry that I might not win the competition. That platform turned me into a new person. It was like I was no longer human. I was spitting words as though I was voicing fire! I was fierce, commanding, and compelling. My speech was instructive and inspiring. When I was done, not only did the audience clap as they did for every other speaker, some of them were on their feet. I did not read any meaning to it. I just felt they enjoyed my speech, as I went back to my seat.

When all the contestants finished speaking, the time came for the judges to tell us how we fared. One of the judges came and summarised everyone's speech and told us how awesome a night it had been. Again, my thoughts about how the first or the second speaker did exceptionally well and there was no way in the world I was winning. When she was done appraising all the speeches, she said, 'Now it's time for us to know how the contestants ranked, and the winner for tonight'. She started from the second runner up for the night and I didn't hear my name. I had thought at least I should be the second runner up if they considered my speech worthy of a prize. No, it wasn't me that was called, it was the second speaker- the young lady who spoke so eloquently. Within me, I said 'I knew it'. And then the first runner-up got called and I still did not hear my name. I said to myself, 'That's it. I am not winning anything tonight'. I started to console myself with uplifting words. You know those internal speeches you give yourself after you have just failed. I was saying things like 'At least, I tried. It was better to fail than not to have tried'. The person that was called was the young man who spoke on the topic 'In pursuit of happiness'. I said to myself, 'Wow! Well deserved' I should mention at this time that I didn't think I was better than those two, so I wasn't having any interesting thoughts other than 'Can we just know who the winner is so we can celebrate the person?"

All of a sudden, I felt my heart racing. A strange thought ran through my mind and it was that, "what if you win this thing?" I immediately brushed it off. I had all the disqualifying reasons why it would not be me including the fact that it was an international toastmasters' event, the audience may not have heard me clearly as I was the only African amongst the contestants. I was sure I was not going to win but the thoughts won't leave me and all of a sudden, I heard 'And the winner for tonight is: Samuel Ekundayo'! My heart skipped a beat. I was both stunned and shocked. For the first time in my life, I had no words. As a sanguine who is naturally full of energy with a lot to say, I was speechless. I shed a tear. It was unbelievable. My friends did not believe I would win so only one of them came. I was called to the podium to receive my prize and certificate and still could not believe it.

I will never forget the words of the judge who called my name. She said, 'All speakers communicate but great speakers inspire...' Those words echo in my heart years after. I realised I had a gift to inspire my world. I also realised my greatness as a speaker is tied to my ability to inspire. Looking through the eyes of everyone present at that Lecture Theatre that night, it was as though they were beholding a Master at his arts. I was sure they were looking at a star right before their very own eyes. When that judge asked for another round of applause as I was asked to step up to the stage, I could see it in their eyes.

As I stepped on the stage to get my prize and certificate, the awareness that I had a gift to inspire couldn't have been more conspicuous. It was so clear to me that God has given me the ability to communicate quite effectively with the world. From that day I began to use that gift intentionally. The only problem was I was not sure about the exact purpose of the gift. So, I was dabbling into all kinds of things. From Radio DJ to Comedy and Master of Ceremonies. Everyone I've helped to handle their ceremonies has felt at one time or the other that I was born to do it because I did it very well.

I could go on and on to tell you about my different gifts and how I came about their realisations and discoveries in my life, but I don't want to bore you because I know you have your own stories too. If you are reading this book, I am guessing it's because we have multi-giftedness in common. What I really would like to communicate to you in this chapter is that despite the many gifts I still felt unsettled and I will tell you why in the next chapter. There was a problem and that problem created a void that lasted for quite some years in my life. I am sure you would be able to relate to this void. Let's go to the next chapter.

Chapter 2:

THE REAL PROBLEM

I admit that the blessings of being multi-gifted are quite numerous and amazing. In fact, let's look at why God gave us so many talents because I believe if we know why we might begin to understand how to navigate the challenge of our multi-giftedness quite intently.

Why we have gifts or talents

God does not waste resources. Nothing about God is wasteful. He is very intentional in everything He does, which means the gifts He has given to us are quite intentional. As a result, I consider the gifts God has given me as an investment of God into my life. For instance, my ability to dance, teach, communicate effectively, act, do graphics design, etc., was very intentional by God. The Bible says, 'In his grace, God has given us different gifts for doing certain things well...'[3] God has given us different gifts for doing certain things well. So, without a doubt, God is quite intentional about your ability to do different things very well. Every ability you have is a responsibility. You must see every gift that God has given to you as a means of expressing His nature on earth.

Another way to look at this is to see it from the perspective of potential. God is a God of potential. We are also full of

---

3   Romans 12:6 NLT

potential. There are things God wants us to do and as long as we're alive, there is always more to do, and this is why God has given us gifts in His grace to do those things, and do them well. If God has given you the ability to write, sing, and speak at the same time, rest assured God wants you to use all of these gifts and quite effectively too so you can maximise your potentials and give Him all the glory as you manifest those gifts

The parable of the talents[4] does justice to this. The Bible records the parable as it relates to the Kingdom of Heaven. It was described as that of a man who was going on a long trip and committed some money into the care of his three servants. We were told that 'he gave five bags of silver to one, two bags of silver to another, and one bag of silver to the last—**dividing it in proportion to their abilities**. He then left on his trip'[5] The man who went on the long trip can be likened to God. His trip relays our journey here on earth with Jesus' imminent second coming. When He comes back, we would give an account of the gifts He gave to us.

That's not what I really wanted to point us to, even though that is very important but I will get to it later. What I would really like to show you was how He divided the money in proportion to their abilities. We can therefore conclude that God gave you all the gifts you have because He knows you can handle them. You have the capacity to handle the responsibility of your many gifts. This is why I congratulate you for picking up this book because you will be able to understand how to navigate these gifts so that you can maximise your potential and do it effectively.

Like the money given to those servants, our gifts were given to us to invest. We're to trade with what we've been given. In fact, we are to trade with all of them. In other words, there is a purpose for all the gifts we have been given. The beginning

---

4   Matthew 25:
5   Matthew 25:15

of effectively utilising the gifts God has given to you is to know the purpose for which they were given. If you don't know the purpose of your gifts, you will struggle!

If you don't know the purpose of your gifts, you will struggle!

Our gifts are given to us as part of our function. Everything God created has a purpose and for that purpose to be fulfilled, its functions were built in. Your gifts were built into you for you to effectively fulfil God's purpose for your life. Take this as the foundation for the solution to the thesis of this book. I will go deeper into it in chapter four but before I conclude this chapter, I need to show you the difference between your gifts and your purpose.

The difference between your gifts and calling

It is a dangerous mindset to think your gifts are the ultimate things about you. It's dangerous to think there is nothing higher or greater than your gifts or talents. In other words, expressing all your gifts is not all there is to living life to the fullest. There is something more to you than your gift and is more important than your gifts. I am bold to say your gifts were given to you for a specific purpose. Until you know the purpose of your gifts, you may misuse and abuse the gift. This is why Myles Munroe said that 'When the purpose of a thing is not known, abuse is inevitable'. If you buy a car and don't understand the purpose of the car, you will abuse the car, no matter how expensive the car is.

In fact, you can't quite maximise a gift if you don't know its purpose. Some years ago, I adopted a young lady as my sister. Her parents were very dear to me. One day, I decided I was going to buy her a phone. I must say at this time, I was a student.

Literally, about 80% of my income was going into paying my study loan and a larger part of the remaining 20% was for my transport to and from school. Nonetheless, I squeezed out a couple of hundred bucks to buy this young lady a phone. I remember that I had not used a brand-new phone myself before then. My phones were usually well-used and looked after second-hand types. So, I bought the phone and gave it to her. I saw how ecstatic she was, and I was so happy.

Some weeks later, the young lady was using the phone while I was at their place and I noticed a crack on the screen of the phone. I had been using my second-hand phone for ages yet no screen crack. I valued my phone so much I had to buy a screen protector and a case to ensure it never cracked. However, this young lady was careless with her phone because she probably had no idea what it cost to give her the phone as a gift, and the purpose for which the gift was given. When I asked her about it, her response was clear: she had no idea.

Many of us are like that. We have gifts but do not know the purpose. We can sing but do not know why. We can write but do not know why, so we just write. Like me, I knew I could communicate but had no idea for years and was just dabbling into a lot of things including comedy, master of ceremonies, radio DJ, etc.

I have come to realise that when a gift is not used for the purpose for which it was given, fulfilment and true satisfaction never truly takes place. Fulfilment only comes from purpose, not from the use of gifts alone. IN 2011, Amy Winehouse, a very famous and exceptionally talented musician, died of alcohol poisoning. She had the gift, was known by her gift but abused the gift. In fact, it was the success of the gift that lured her into the abuse of her body and life. Records show that she had turned to alcohol in the wake of any success and was often too drunk to perform several times such that her fans would boo her off the stage, and some of her tours would get cancelled as a result. Again, when the purpose is not known, abuse is inevitable. Please, do not be consumed by your many gifts that you are not bothered to know the reason you have been blessed with such gifts.

In my opinion, gifts are a measure of responsibility. When we know the purpose of our gifts, we understand the responsibility or in the words of Paul the Apostle, the 'necessity'[6] laid on us to fulfil God's purpose with our gifts. You will not just be comfortable 'performing' with your gifts, you will be more pre-occupied by the purpose of the gifts such that you will be responsible. Paul the Apostle knew his ability to communicate amidst his many other gifts was for the sole purpose of preaching the gospel and he knew how vital this was to his fulfilment, meaning, impact, influence, and significance in life. You too must recognise that your gifts were given to you for a specific purpose, calling, and assignment.

Apart from that, if you use the gift and forget the giver of the gift, you will abuse the gift. So many people maximise their talents and as a result, become famous. Their fame then causes them to lose sight of the giver of the gift. No matter how well you use the gift, if you fail to honour the giver of the gift, you are an ingrate and an ingrate has no place in the heart of anyone. No wonder the Bible says, 'Remember the LORD your God. He is the one who gives you power to be successful, in order to fulfil the covenant he confirmed to your ancestors with an oath'[7]. There are a few things we must note about this scripture.

---

6   1 Corinthians 9:16 (ESV) - For if I preach the gospel, that gives me no ground for boasting. For necessity is laid upon me. Woe to me if I do not preach the gospel!
7   Deuteronomy 3:18 NLT

1. Remember the Lord your God – the giver! God gave you all that you have today. God gave you your many abilities.

2. The word 'power' in the scripture is actually from the Hebrew word *'kôach'* which means ability, passion. So, it's reminding us to remember the God that gave us our special abilities and talents.

3. The WHY! Every gift has a WHY. The purpose of the abilities is stated in the scripture. It says '...**in order to fulfil** the covenant he confirmed to your ancestors with an oath'.

Let's summarise, shall we?

Your abilities were given to you to fulfil God's purpose for your life. You cannot forget the giver of the gift while you use His gift. The gift was not yours, you were given so you must honour the giver. Aside from that, you must use the gift as it was intended to be used, otherwise, you will abuse it. Another scripture says, 'Don't let the excitement of youth cause you to forget your Creator. Honour him in your youth before you grow old and say, "Life is not pleasant anymore."'[8]. The best way to honour God is to use your gifts to honour Him and to fulfil His purpose for your life.

Your abilities were given to you to fulfil God's purpose for your life

Don't be a successful failure

If you fail to use your gifts for the purpose for which you were given or fail to honour your creator, then, the best you can be

---

8   Ecclesiastes 12:1 NLT

is a successful failure. A successful failure is someone the world thinks is a success but in the eyes of God is a failure.

I am a lecturer and I would like to illustrate this using an example of a student of mine some years back. Let's call his name Henry. You see, Henry was a 55-year-old man at the time. He was almost the same age as my Dad when he was in my class. Every time I gave an assignment in class, Henry would contest it. He always had better ways I could have set the question, presented it to the class, or asked the student to approach it. After every class, Henry would come into my office to present his arguments on why he thought I was wrong.

Several times, I wouldn't respond to Henry's argument. I would just be quiet. I believe Henry took my silence or a few words for conceding defeat. So, Henry would go do the assignment just the way he wanted to do it. He would do the assignment excellently according to his own requirements, not mine (the lecturer's) I believe one of the most dangerous ways to live life is to live it according to your own requirements and not your creator's. It's too risky. I always ensured I gave Henry zero marks. I didn't spare him at all. I wanted to teach him a lesson, and it was that, despite his other ideas about my assignment, I am still the lecturer and I have the full rights to the requirements of the assignment. His concerns and arguments cannot change the requirements.

The assignments were given weekly for about five weeks and every week, Henry would do the same thing – come to my office after I'd dished out the assignments to the students to argue about why I didn't set the questions correctly, presented them to the class poorly or how I could have asked the students to approach the assignment differently. For four weeks in a row, Henry got zero marks. After the class before the final assessment in those five weeks, Henry stormed into my office as usual but this time he was very calm. I noticed he was not in the mood to argue. He was not puffed up, arrogant, or in his usual corrective mood. He was humbler and sober. The first words that came out of his mouth shocked me. Henry said, 'Dr Samuel, I have just realised something'. I asked 'What is that?' Henry replied, 'I'm not supposed to be arguing with my Lecturer right?' I responded, 'I think so'. Henry left my office that day without arguing with me. He had made a life-changing realisation, that no matter how old and experienced he was, the most important thing, if he was going to be successful in his assignments, was to follow the requirements of the Lecturer, and not his.

Henry went home that day and did the assignment this time, not according to his own requirements but mine. When I got Henry's papers, you could see he was quite conscientious and intentional about following my requirements. That brought smiles to my face. I knew Henry had finally gotten it. I gave him full marks. When he got his results, he rushed to my office and said, 'Thank you'! I smiled.

Life is like a school. God is the lecturer, and we are the students. We cannot be too smart for God. Even if we think we are, our assignments must be done according to His requirements, not how we think it should be done. To live your life based on how you deem right, and not according to the dictate of God is to set yourself on the path of failure. To do excellently what you have not been asked to do is to live as a successful failure. In the end, like Henry, you will still get zero marks until you decide to repent and change your ways.

Your gifts and talents were given to you for a specific purpose with specific requirements from the giver – your creator and maker. To think you are smart and try to tweak the requirements is to set yourself up for failure. The use of your gifts must honour your marker and it must fulfil His requirements.

That way you will delight Him and He will release more grace for you to do more and live a fulfilled and meaningful life.

But if you choose to do things your own way and use your gifts however you deem it fit to use, then you will run into problems. In the next section, I will expatiate on some of these problems you will run into or maybe you are already in.

So, what are these problems?

There are many issues with not knowing how to leverage your many gifts. If you are not careful, you will never maximise your potential. I am reminded of the words of the late Dr Myles Munroe who was always fond of saying, 'The richest place on earth is not the oil fields of the middle east or the gold mines of Africa. The richest place on earth is the graveyard because many people have died with their potentials untapped – with books they could have written but never wrote, songs they could have sung but no one heard, businesses that could have changed the world but never saw the light of day and so on'.

I believe we all must maximise our potential if we want to live a fulfilled life and not regret it in the afterlife. In the words of Rick Warren, in his book, *Purpose-Driven Life: What on earth am I here for*, when we get to see God, He will most likely ask us two questions: the first is, *what did you do with Jesus Christ?* This is a question of salvation – that will most likely guarantee your access to heaven. The second question is: *what did you do with all I gave you?* This is a question of accountability. As I said earlier, God does not waste resources. Everything He has given us, we will account for. While we must use all that God has given to us for His glory, it is important we know how to maximise them, so we can be faithful stewards because misuse or abuse of them will result in problems including the ones I'll be sharing in subsequent sections.

The most apparent evidence of the misuse or abuse of your multi-talents is the lack of value. Our gifts were given to us to make us people of worth and value. Value speaks of the relative worth, utility, or importance of something. The dictionary says it's the 'monetary worth or market price of something'[9]. While I do not just want to base this on monetary terms alone, I must mention it is significant. People who have learned to maximise their gifts are always valuable monetarily, and this is germane to the solution I present in this book.

If you are a jack of all trades and not a master of anything, there is a likelihood you will not be paid much. In fact, your only payment would be people's envy of all you possess in terms of talents and not your monetary value. People don't pay potential, they only pay mastery. Until you're known for something, you will never be valuable, meaning that people won't pay you.

People don't pay potential, they only pay mastery

This was my story for many years of my life. I was good at many things, but I didn't attract money, no one was paying me until I moved from potential to mastery. They were calling me to do all kinds of things – Master of Ceremony, dance performance, comedy, resolve technical and IT problems, create websites and design graphics, etc. but my value and worth were still very low. This is why you cannot afford that life. It's tiring. If you don't journey towards mastery, all you will get is misery, no matter how gifted you are. God has not designed you and given you all those gifts for you to live a miserable life.

---

9   Merriam Webster Dictionary - https://www.merriam-webster.com/dictionary/value

It's dangerous to lack value here on earth and also not to be valuable to heaven.

Lack of effectiveness

A lack of mastery of your gifts would make you ineffective. People will be calling you for all kinds of things. You will be all over the place. You will be very busy. Unfortunately, because you have not mastered any of those gifts, you will not be effective. You will just be making motion yet no progress. People will just see you as someone they can use whenever they want. The apparent lack of value will make people not value you as well. They will be able to see through your ineffectiveness and would not want to commit anything to you.

Results are what guarantee effectiveness. In other words, results follow mastery not just being busy. Don't live life like a rocking chair making so much motion and consuming so much energy but stuck on one spot and not going anywhere. God does not like ineffective people. We could see that in the Parable of the Talents. He was crossed with the guy who had nothing to show for his talent, he referred to him as 'wicked'.

The False Genius Syndrome

I have also discovered that when you don't know how to maximise your gifts, you are likely to be stuck in a zone of false genius. I call it false genius because it is possible to be average at that very thing you are good at. While people are hailing and praising you as a genius as a result of your multi-giftedness, you will feel something is missing, but you may not be able to own up to it because of the apparent pride people's praises bring to you. Yes, pride – feeling like you are now wanted by people. Pride will make you stuck in that zone if you are not careful. Instead of developing yourself, growing, and becoming all you could be, you will be enjoying people's praises at the expense of your greatness.

To be very frank, the zone of false genius for the multi-talented individual comes with a veil that blocks you from seeing you are not valuable yet if you haven't learnt how to refine and maximise your gifts. The praise of men won't let you see clearly. Pride often creates the illusion that you are a star, and that is why you are being praised and seemingly needed by people. Don't fall for that. There is more outside of your false genius zone. More that will require a journey from misery to mastery and that will cost you. It will cost you a lot of things. We will talk about this cost in another chapter.

The General Practitioner Syndrome: Lack of uniqueness

Some years back, a colleague of mine had a throat infection and it was so bad it didn't answer to antibiotics and other prescriptions by her local General Practitioner (GP). After a while, when it appeared that things were getting worse, the GP had to refer her to a throat specialist. In fact, I remember, before she could get an appointment with the specialist, it took a while. When she eventually got it, she needed to pay around $600 an hour to see the specialist. Whether she'll spend the whole hour or not, it didn't matter, she had to pay that money for her first hour with the specialist. From memory, that $600 was even subsidised by the government, otherwise, she'd be paying more than a thousand bucks. Why am I sharing this with you?

Have you ever been to a GP before? How much did you pay per visit? On the other hand, have you ever had to see a specialist for anything? Can you compare how much you paid your GP with what you had to pay the specialist? GPs don't earn what specialists earn. In fact, I had to do some research into this even though my wife is a medical doctor and I've asked her a lot. One of the websites I consulted had this to say, 'Specialists earn almost twice as much as GPs but only half of this difference can be explained by differences in their characteristics'[10]. The GPs referred to in that column are consultant GPs (more advanced GPs), which means, ideally, specialists earn way more than most GPs. Why is this important?

People don't value generalists that much and it reflects in their monetary worth. This is what I call the GP syndrome. Please don't be caught up in being a generalist. To be multi-gifted and not know what to do with all your gifts can make you a generalist such that you never become a master of your gifts. I'll talk about the solution to this in the next chapter.

Lack of influence or leadership

God created us to be leaders and authorities in different spheres of life. While all we've been given were given to help us become authorities and leaders, we cannot become so in a very ineffective way. There is an area of life you were born to lead in and trying to put all your eggs in a basket at the same time won't let you assume your throne.

Greatness is not found in the misery that comes with being the jack of all trade. Leadership is the capacity to influence people such that they follow you without coercion. If you fail to recognise how to maximise your gifts, you will lack influence, and if you are not careful, despite how gifted you are, you will die ordinary. Many heroes have died unsung and undiscovered as a result of this. Don't be one of them. This is why I wrote this book for you.

---

10 https://www.racgp.org.au/afp/2014/april/
does-remuneration-matter/

If you fail to recognise how to maximise your gifts, you will lack influence, and if you are not careful, despite how gifted you are, you will die ordinary

Lack of fulfilment

The Merriam Websiter[11] dictionary defines 'fulfil' in many ways including, 'to meet the requirements of...', 'to measure up to...', 'to bring to an end...', 'to develop the full potentialities of...' If you look at these definitions, you would realise the fact that they are all corresponding to an earlier established order, a requirement, or purpose. Whether it is to meet the requirements of an established order, or to measure up to an established order or standard, to bring to an end or complete something that had been set earlier, or to develop the full potentialities of a product, which is what we often refer to as maximising potentials; it is clear something had been established for us to bring 'fulfilment' into the picture.

One of the worst ways to live life is to not be mindful of fulfilment. It is to fail to realise that there was an established order over your life before you got to planet earth. It is to diminish the importance of the requirements laid out for you to meet with your life. Failing to learn how to maximise your gifts may cost you your fulfilment. You will never be able to develop to the full potentialities of your gifts if you just use them anyhow. The misuse or abuse of your gifts will never bring you fulfilment. If you are not careful, the very thing designed to be a blessing may be your curse. We don't want that.

---

11   Merriam Webster Dictionary - https://www.merriam-webster. com/dictionary/fulfill

So, what is the solution to these problems, you ask? How can I maximise my gifts and multi-talents? How can I become the jack of a trade and live a fulfilled life? I've got you. We will discuss the solution in the next chapter. Are you ready?

Chapter 3

THE SOLUTION

God does not waste resources. All He has given to you were given to you because you need them to fulfil His purpose for your life. He is an intentional God. To help you live fulfilled, He has laid out some principles to help you live effectively. He doesn't want you to live miserably. He wants you to be valuable. I want to share with you in this chapter the practical keys to help you maximise your gifts and consequently maximise your potentials.

Discover your purpose/calling

As I said earlier, your gifts were given to you for a purpose. To not know the purpose of a gift is to misuse, abuse, or not value the gift. But when you know the purpose of a gift, you will value and look after it.

When God was creating you, He had the very thing(s) He wanted you to come and do here all figured out. You see, God thought about you long and hard enough and created you intentionally to meet a need here on earth. This is why He deposited everything you have within you to help you complete your assignment. Picture with me a car and the many functions inside a car. From the gears in the engine to the tyres on its four sides, from the steering wheel providing direction to the car to the accelerator that dictates the speed of the car per time, you would notice that the multi-functions of the car was for the main purpose of moving people from one destination to the other. No matter how beautiful the interior of a car is, if it fails to move from one spot, the value and effectiveness of the car would disappear.

I have some friends who value classic cars. I don't. I just don't like old things. I always prefer the latest technology and things. I have come to realise that the value of those classic cars is in their abilities to get them moving. If no one can get them to work – that is, move from one place to another – that car in all of its beauty and essence would remain parked or wrecked eventually. While the parked car may serve other purposes, that's not the intended purpose by the manufacturer. While the gears and other parts of the car could be removed and used for other things, it would not be as fulfilling as using them for their originally intended purpose of use. Like the car, you also have all the many gifts you have so you can fulfil a specific purpose. No matter the number of things you do so well, your gifts will be abused, misused and undervalued, if you fail to discover the very purpose for which you were given those gifts.

It was the year 2016 and I had been feeling the void within that I spoke about earlier for several years since completing my Ph.D. One day, I heard a preacher speak from the Bible. In the book of Luke 12:48, the Bible says, '...*For everyone to whom much is given, from him much will be required; and to whom much has been committed, of him they will ask the more*.' The preacher spoke with so much impetus that I could feel every word. The whole time, I was under the influence of his voice. It felt as though he was screaming those words straight into my ears. He said, 'Everything God has given you, your gifts, your talents, your knowledge, your wisdom, your wealth, and so on, you will give account to Him. God does not waste resources and you will have to account for what you did with all you have been given'. I went back home and couldn't sleep for days. I knew God was talking to me. I was very guilty. Up until that time, I had been using my gifts anyhow with no knowledge of the purpose of the gifts. Realising I would give an account became a scary thing for me. I just knew I could not go on living like that. I had to do something about it.

Some days later, I decided I was going to go on a few days fast with one singular focus. I was only going to pray a single prayer – Lord, why have you given me these gifts? I was asking God for my purpose and the purpose of the many talents I had. I was no longer comfortable just living anyhow. I was no longer comfortable in my false genius. I was determined to become a person of value because I would give account and I wanted to make sure God saw me as a faithful steward of all He has given me. I do hope that this book brings such realisation to you as well.

On one of the days of my fasting and praying, God spoke to me quite audibly. He said, 'Help people discover their purpose'. WOW! I wrote it down and my life has since changed. I walked out of that prayer time with God feeling brand new. That was how 'The Purpose Preacher' was born! I had been born again before, but I felt like I became born again, again! No wonder Mark Twain said, 'The two most important days in your life are the day you are born and the day you find out why'. If you ever find out why you were born, I promise you, you will feel brand new! The feeling is beyond what I can put into words. I decided that day that I was going to live my life helping others find their purpose. It was very clear that all the gifts God deposited inside of me were to help people discover their purpose, but which one? I will answer this question in the next section because there is a key principle I need to share with you in it.

Find your dominant gift(s)

In his book, The Law of Recognition, Mike Murdock said, 'You may have many gifts, but to succeed in life, you should place your full concentration on your dominant gift'. While you are good at many things, not all of them will bring value to you. In fact, there are some things we call gifts that we are quite just better than average in and are not excellent at.

For instance, I love to dance but when I see some gifted people dance, I realise that my ability to dance isn't quite a gift but mere passion. Understanding the concept of a dominant gift will help you realise that some of the things you do so well are not gifts so to speak. If you watch American Idol or Britain's Got Talent, or any of these talent quest shows, you will understand what I'm driving at. You will see people who think they can sing and then they get on stage, you're wondering where and who lied to them. It's not because they can't quite hold a tune or pick the right key or sing on the beat or rhythm, but others do it so well that it becomes obvious that these other people were not built for it.

Your most dominant gifts are the ones that empower you to shine so easily, it feels you're supremely and divinely qualified to do or express them. This reminds me of the scripture that says, 'In his grace, God has given us different gifts for doing certain things well...'[12] All of us have grace in an area of life to do certain things well, or should I dare say, without trying to add to God's word, we all have the grace to do certain things very well. The word 'well' in Greek is transliterated as 'more excellent' or 'unique'. Meaning, this is something you do so excellently, perhaps more than anyone you know. No matter when you're called upon to do it, whether it is in the morning, afternoon, or night, you are fired up and ready to go. It's inbuilt. You're graced and engineered for it.

12   Romans 12:6 NLT

Your most dominant gifts are the ones that empower you to shine so easily, it feels you're supremely and divinely qualified to do or express them

When you do that thing, you will know you are excellent at it. You will almost feel you are the best, without deceiving yourself. I said that because many people deceive themselves, they know they are not built for something but because at one time or the other some people have praised them about it, they feel 'that's it'. No! It may not be it. This reminds me of King Saul in the Old Testament. There were a few times that he prophesied. Does that mean he was a prophet? No! I remember the first account of his prophecy, Samuel declared over him the following:

'After that thou shalt come to the hill of God, where is the garrison of the Philistines: and it shall come to pass, when thou art come thither to the city, that thou shalt meet a company of prophets coming down from the high place with a psaltery, and a tabret, and a pipe, and a harp, before them; and they shall prophesy: And the Spirit of the Lord will come upon thee, and thou shalt prophesy with them, and shalt be turned into another man'[13]

Even though Saul prophesied at those times, as spoken of by the Prophet of God, it was no indication that Prophecy was Saul's dominant gift. In fact, it was more or less a temporary gift. The next time Saul tried to take the place of the prophet of God (Samuel) due to his impatience, he decided he could do the burnt offering all by himself. This probably was because he had just prophesied a few chapters ago, he thought he could just function in any office as he likes, and whenever he likes. What he did cost him. In fact, he lost his entire kingdom as a

---

13   1Samuel 10:5-6 KJV

result. This is why I always say, trying to function in anything you are not graced to do is setting yourself up for disgrace. The best place to function for God's grace to flow through you and for you to be an embodiment of His glory is in an area you are graced in. Please don't be like Saul. Know what you are graced to do and stick to the plan.

I know you're now asking, 'Dr Sam, so, how do I know my dominant gift'? I'm glad you asked. I have what I call the Dominant Gift(s) Test.

The Dominant Gift(s) Test

TEST 1: Can you function in that gift and get consistent results?

If you can, then it is most likely your dominant gift. That's the test. If you function in something you call your gift and yet cannot produce consistent results, then it may not be your dominant gift. It could be a gift but it's not the dominant one.

For me, my most dominant gift is my ability to communicate. When I speak, I feel like I'm in my zone of genius! As a result, I produce consistent results in my speaking, especially when I'm speaking about something I'm very passionate about, for instance, the topic of purpose. I could speak for five hours non-stop to you about your purpose and not feel tired. I would even forget that I have not had lunch or dinner. Apart from that, my ability to communicate is my superpower because God has used it in transforming many lives. As a coach, I've coached many people and helped them discover or clarify their purpose such that they leave my sessions feeling empowered and ready to live life brand new! This is why people pay me for clarity sessions, monthly coaching, and attend my masterclasses because they know they will get results. My speaking is a gift that has produced consistent results over the years and is still doing so till today. Do you have a gift, amongst your many gifts, that brings transformation in people's lives too? That is also most likely your most dominant gift.

TEST 2: Do you want to be the best at it?

If it is your dominant gift, you would want to be the best at it. When I talk about being the best, I don't necessarily mean competing with others. I mean, that you want to be better today than you were yesterday. You're never satisfied with mediocrity or average results. As a result, there is a yearning inside of you to do more, be more, and give more. This desire will fuel inside of you a passion for learning and growth. You will just realise, without anyone forcing it on you or coercing you, that you are signing up for courses, seminars, masterclasses, and coaching programmes just to make sure you are the best you can be.

This is why even the best sportsmen and women in the world have coaches. Their coaches may not be as good as them in the sports but the desire to be great requires that you constantly grow, develop, and refine your gifts and this is what a coach does for and with you. If a gift is your superpower, the desire to be the best you can be will always be there. It will wake you up every morning. You will not be comfortable being average. Deep within, you would know you could be more! More will be calling out to you. This is why I don't stop learning. In the next section, I will share with you more on the power of refining that gift and focusing on it to become the person of value that is sought-after in your generation and the ones to come.

When I took this test, I realised there are two key areas where I get consistent results and that I want to be the best in. Those areas for me are speaking and writing. Since making this discovery, I decided to write and speak every day. Speaking is my primary zone of genius. When I speak, I get results, lives get transformed, and I feel fulfilled. Also, I passionately desire to grow my speaking ability. I am always learning, always practising, always seeking to be better. I am always listening to great orators and attempting some of their tips and tricks that work. I am very keen on developing the art of speaking despite the fact that it's a gift for me. This gift comes very handy in my coaching business.

TEST 3: Do you feel like you are supernatural when performing that thing?

In my book, Purpose in Crisis, I shared a powerful insight I think every child of God must know in it. I call it 'The Dimension of God on Your Inside'. Sometime ago, God showed me this revelation from the Bible where He said, '*And the LORD God formed man of the dust of the ground and breathed into his nostrils the breath of life; and man became a living soul*'[14] The word 'breath' in Hebrew is transliterated as '*neshâmâh*' which means *divine inspiration*. There is an inspiration of God in every man that came with them since creation or birth.

When I read that scripture and was meditating on it, I remember asking God, 'Lord, did you put your entire self into the man'? and I heard God say, 'No, I didn't put my entire self into the man. If I did, that man would become another 'God'. What I did was put a part of myself into every man'. I came out of that prayer time with a powerful realisation. I realised that there is a dimension of God's inspiration in every man.

What is the meaning of this literally? It means there is something you know how to do at the level of 'God'! Absolutely! There is an ability of God inside of you that allows you to perform through direct inspiration from the Spirit of God. In fact, this is the meaning of the term GRACE. Grace is the power or ability of God at work in a human being that enables him to produce God-like results. The dimension of God in your life is where God's grace is at its peak!

---

14   Genesis 2:7 KJV

Grace is the power or ability of God at work in a human being that enables him to produce God-like results. The dimension of God in your life is where God's grace is at its peak!

This means if the dimension of God in your life is speaking, when you speak, people will hear God speak, not you. If the dimension of God in you is music when you sing or play instruments, you are not the one being seen or heard, you are just a loudspeaker for the one singing or performing through you – GOD. If yours is in the area of cooking when you cook, you are not the one cooking, it is God cooking through you. This is why no matter how hard you try to teach people this dimension of God in you, they can never do it like you. They can try so hard, but it will never be like the way you do it. The reason is that what a man does by grace, no one can do by trying hard.

What I am saying, in essence, is that your most dominant gift is an area of life where you have the ability of God! So, while you may have many talents and gifts, please look out for that one that produces God-like results when you do it. That's the one you should focus on, or at least start building your brand on. I will talk more about personal branding in one of the subsequent sections.

Mastery – Focus and Refinement

Taking the test and identifying your zone(s) of genius is just the beginning. To maximise your dominant gifts, you have to learn the art of focus and refinement. I'll start with focus.

In the early days of my career after university, I wrote on my curriculum vitae (CV) these exact words, *'I am an excellent multitasker with the ability to juggle many things at a high level of precision and accuracy'*. If you had seen my CV then, you would see those exact words in there. I didn't know I was undoing myself. The truth is, it is impossible to be productive and effective at anything without focusing on that thing. Neuroscientists and psychologists have found that it is impossible for humans to multitask. In fact, when we say we're multitasking, what we're doing is stopping one thing to do another. No one can multitask and be effective.

Focus is key if your gifts will bring value to you. I know it's hard for a multi-talented individual like you to be focused but remember where we started from, you cannot keep making motion without progress or being busy and not be effective. The key to changing all of that is discovering your most dominant gifts and focusing on them.

So many people have challenged this theory of mine and said, 'But look at someone like Bishop T.D. Jakes. He is a pastor, author, film producer, music producer, and so on. He is using all of his multi-talents and he is well known for them'. My answer to such people is, Bishop T.D. Jakes did not start with all of those gifts. Yes! In fact, what brought Bishop Jakes to the limelight was not film production or music production. I want to believe he had those gifts before he became popular but his focus was on his preaching gift first. That was what brought him to the limelight. It was his message 'woman thou art loosed' that was the game-changer for him.

So many of the celebrities who are 'multi-talented' did not become famous for all their gifts. Most of them came into the limelight and got known for just one thing first. It was after they had become known for one thing, that they started bringing out other parts of them and because people trusted them as a brand initially for that one thing, they are easily able to buy into their other gifts.

Your focus is very germane to your value. We live in a world that is full of distractions and they have become the weakness of the majority of the people. Many would rather lavish their time and money on distractions than invest in themselves to become who they were created to be. The key to becoming a person of value is focusing like a laser beam on your most dominant gift. Be known for one thing first, one thing you are very good at, one thing you are supremely and divinely qualified to do, one thing you have the grace of God backing you up in.

Let's bring it home. What is the value of focusing on your most dominant gift(s)? Focus is the key to productivity and effectiveness. It means to put all your energy into one task until you see it to fruition. This means, pour your entire life into your most dominant gift and do not let all other gifts be a distraction until you have built something solid and worthwhile with your most dominant gift. This is why it is key to understand the science of personal branding. As a coach, I help my clients build a personal brand around their most dominant gift(s) till they become highly sought-after and paid as a result.

The most annoying thing about distractions is that they are very attractive, and this is what makes focus very hard. How can you abandon many attractive things to focus on only one attractive thing? It's like you're missing out, right? Anything that commands your focus is attractive and I tell you, the very things you are not supposed to focus on will always attract you but you cannot afford to give in.

This focus is not forever by the way. Once you have built an effective personal brand and people can trust your prowess with your most dominant gift, then you can begin to diversify. The trust in the brand you've built for your most dominant gifts will help you build other brands later. I know you're asking, so how do I build a personal brand around my most dominant gifts? Don't worry, I've got you. I will show you in the next section but first, let me talk about refinement.

Refinement

All gifts, including your most dominant gifts, were given to us crude and raw. They have to be refined for you to be able to maximise them. Don't let anyone fool you and make you think because God graced you with it, then you don't have to refine it. You will be making a grave mistake. Just like gold or diamond discovered in the rough, its potential is massive but until it goes through the refiner's fire, that potential may never be realised. To fail to refine your gift is to waste it.

So, how do you refine your gift? Like what fire does to gold to make it valuable, so do learning and growth to make your gifts more valuable. While I'm a gifted speaker, I've had to learn and grow my speaking. I've had to learn the art of speaking, of storytelling, of engaging with my audience, of selling on and off stage, and so on. In learning the art of speaking, I became aware of the power of stories for my speaking – how to introduce my talks, how to engage people's feelings and emotions in my speech, how and when to look straight into their eyes, how to make my audience engage with my talk, and so on. These important lessons helped me grow, whereas a crude speaker would just dabble into things and may never get the results expected because of failing to refine his or her gifts. That it is your dominant gift does not mean you cannot learn or be coached by others.

Coaching is another important way of refining your gifts. The champions of the world have coaches. Lionel Messi has a coach,

Cristiano Ronaldo has a coach, Roger Federer, Serena Williams, and so on, and they all require coaches for them to be at the peak of their game. This is so important so they can perform at the peak of their strengths. While teachers teach, coaches improve your performance. If you want to maximise the potential of your most dominant gifts, you have no choice but to invest in a coach or some coaches. I have been very blessed to have worked with some coaches in my life.

When I started as a speaker, my first coach was a man called Grant Baldwin. He taught me how to build a personal brand as a speaker. I learnt so many things from him like, how to ensure I have a website, how to communicate my message to the world, how to make money from my speaking, and so on. It was not cheap. At the time, I couldn't afford it but I also knew I could not afford not to afford it so I had to sacrifice for it. Refining your gift would require that you sacrifice for it. It won't be easy, it will be painful but what is success without sacrifice? No champion ever made it without pain and sacrifice.

Growth is also key to refinement. You must make it a duty to keep growing. In the words of John C. Maxwell, you must have a personal development plan. Yes, every month, you set aside a percentage of your income that you will commit to your growth. Growth is never automatic. Growth is not a function of age, it's a function of sacrifice and service. If you don't have a growth plan, you will never grow. This is the reason why many multitalented individuals end up adding to the wealth of the graveyard because they will never subject themselves to personal development. They allow the praise from men about the performance of their different gifts to get into their heads and they start to think they don't need to learn from anyone. That is a dangerous mindset.

Growth is never automatic. Growth is not a function of age, it's a function of sacrifice and service.

Another key way to refine your gift is to serve it. Service is one word that is gradually disappearing from the vocabulary of our generation. To serve is to be a servant. When people hear this, they say 'it is not my portion in Jesus' name'. The truth is greatness is embedded in service. Greatness does not answer to desire, it answers to service. You can only serve your way to the top. You must serve others with your gift. In fact, one of the ways God helps us to reach the peak of our performance is by putting us through the test of serving others with our gifts. How do you use your dominant gifts in the church? How do you use them at work? Why is this important? The Bible says, 'And if you are not faithful with other people's things, why should you be trusted with things of your own'?[15] The question is very rhetorical. God is saying, no one would commit anything great into your hands unless you have been found faithful serving someone else with your gifts. Stop running away from service. Be the first to put your hand up to serve others with your gift.

By the grace of God, now I preach at least 120 times a year. I remember when I first started and my Pastor gave the assignment of preaching on the radio twice a week. It was tough because the church had paid for a whole year on the radio in advance and the person the church was expecting to do it became busy. So, my pastor called me up and asked if I could step in. I said yes. I had to prepare messages every week. I had to be disciplined to be there on time. I served my gift faithfully. Today, all the things I learnt during that season are now serving me.

---

15   Luke 16:12 NLT

Another way is through practice. The best of the best became the best not just because they're gifted but because they have learnt the value of practice. They develop the winning mentality and attitude through practice. Practice is one of the key ways to gaining mastery of your most dominant gift. When I first started as a speaker, I remember listening to the podcast of Brendon Burchard where he mentioned how he practised his way into extemporaneous speaking (that is, spoken or done without preparation). I loved and welcomed the idea. I said to myself, 'I want to learn how to speak extemporaneously too'. Brendon on that podcast mentioned how for several months, he would practice every day, in front of the mirror, when he was alone, and so on. As a result of his practice, he had developed the gifts so much that when it was time for his video recording with his team, all he needed was a topic to speak on, and without looking at any notes, he would just speak. Indeed, greatness is doing publicly what you have been doing excellently in private.

I learnt from Brendon and I decided I was going to do the same. For months, I would practice in front of the mirror. I would pick a topic and just speak. Sometimes, I would record myself and just speak. I started with five minutes and then it went on to ten. Before I knew it, after several months of practice, I was able to do an hour. Now, whenever I speak, I hardly look through 20% of my notes if I had one. I would just go on and on and people are getting inspired and their lives transformed. In fact, I have had people, I mean speakers, who would come to me in amazement wondering how I'm able to speak with such impetus and audacity without looking at my notes. The key is my months of practicing when no one was looking. Now, let me show you how to build a personal brand around your most dominant gift.

You are a king!

One of the most fascinating things about God's design for our lives is how He sees us as kings. You see, life is a story of a King (God) and His kingdom. In His kingdom, the people are also kings. This is why He is referred to as 'The King of kings'. The Bible says, '**And hath made us kings and priests unto God** and his Father; to him be glory and dominion for ever and ever'[16]. Isn't that interesting?

Every piece of this jigsaw represents the different territories assigned to each man or woman. These territories represent our place of dominion – domain. That's the place of our rule and dominion. I often say that two things make a king – territory and authority. A king is not a king that does not have territory and authority. If such a kind exists, then he doesn't sit on his throne anymore. He has been displaced.

This concept is so important for you to understand as a king. You have a territory given to you by God! Guess what? You only have authority in that territory of your gift. Outside your

---

16   Revelations 1:6 KJV

territory, you don't have authority. This means, as long as you stay in your territory, you lead, you rule, you dominate. However, the moment you step out of your territory for whatever reason, you become displaced, thus, you lose your authority, and if you are not careful, you become a slave whereas you are supposed to be ruling. Many people have become slaves when they were made to rule and dominate. They've lost their dominion to addiction, sin, complacency, and competition. Some people have lost their territory because they are trying to compete for someone else's territory. They see someone doing well in their territory and as a result of jealousy and envy, they are trying to displace the other person. In fact, this is one of the major sources of chaos in our world - men and women who are competing with others in their territory. They refuse to discover their territory where they have authority but because of the seduction of success, they become vagabonds and robbers seeking to loot other people's territory. What they do not realise is, you cannot displace a king installed by God. The best you can be in another man's territory is a slave. You may be a decorated slave but that doesn't make you a king. Quit the spirit of competition today and find your place so that you can begin to rule and reign. God is counting on you and generations await your rule over the resources God has put in your care within your territory.

If you look at the Jigsaw closely, you would notice a few things and it's important we discuss this, so you can understand this concept very well.

1. **When a piece is in its rightful place, it fits.**

The meaning of this is, no matter how hard you try, you can never fit in another man's place. In fact, each piece has been cut to fit into its place. One of the major sources of frustration in life is people trying to fit where they do not belong. It's like a square peg trying to fit into a round hole.

While you can try for it to fit, there would sure be bruises, pain, agony, and frustration. However, when you are in your rightful place, everything falls into place without struggle.

2. **When a piece is in its rightful place, it's easier for others around it to find their place**.

God designed the world in such a way that when people find their place, the destinies connected to them find their place very easily too. Your ignorance of your territory is costing so many others, thousands of them, millions of them, their place. This is why it is so vital you find your place because of the many destinies connected to you. When you find your place, those people will easily understand the picture and as a result, they would locate where they belong. This is what makes the world beautiful. The other side of this is when you fail to find your place, all of the destinies connected to you will struggle. Some of them will give up because you fail to find your place. Some of them will quit their race because of your ignorance of your place or your disobedience in refusing to find and stay in your place. Never forget that there are destinies connected to you and you will give an account when you get to heaven. So, find your place and begin to rule, reign and lead.

3. **The picture is beautiful when all the pieces find their place**

When our kids were much younger, they used to love puzzles. I am not very patient to put puzzles together, so I would just watch and admire their tenacity, especially my eldest son. He would in no time put the puzzles together and I'll be amazed! What I often notice is the beauty of the picture when all the pieces find their place on the puzzle and well linked together. You could easily see the animals, the house, or whatever the puzzle was. It was always a beautiful sight. This is exactly what life would be like when you find your place and help others find their places too. Life becomes beautiful. From you discovering your purpose, exercising your dominant gifts, and using them to add value to others, you become effective and valuable, as a result, you can reach more people, help them find their place, and they too go ahead to help others find their places. Oh, what a beautiful world! Are you seeing what I'm seeing? This is how God intended for the world to be. Each of us in our rightful place as kings of our territories with legal authority from God to lead, rule, and reign. How beautiful!

Build your personal brand around it.

If you have identified your place and are ruling as the king that you are, and created to be, then I have to show you a principle that is very important to help you become known for what you do. That principle is called personal branding.

I first came about the term personal branding quite comprehensively sometime in 2016. I became aware that everyone has a personal brand but very few personal brands are quite effective. I started to learn how to build an effective personal brand, especially around my most dominant gifts and that was the game-changer for me.

Allow me to define a personal brand for you. **A personal brand is a widely recognised and largely uniform perception or impression of an individual based on their experience, expertise, competencies, actions, and/or achievements within their domain**. There are some keywords in that definition. The first is 'widely recognised'. Your brand must be widely recognised. The goal is to be known for that thing you are building your brand on. I believe an effective personal brand is such that it attracts people to you. When you are a solution, you are supposed to attract the problems you're solving. An effective personal brand attracts the problems it promises the world it's solving. So, you cannot be shy if you are trying to build a brand that will be widely recognised. Your social media handles cannot be set to private if you are trying to build a widely recognised brand. I believe you have to be the light and the salt Jesus refers to in Matthew Chapter 5. Light cannot be hidden, so you cannot afford to be hidden. You cannot be private with the solution you bring to the world if you are going to build an effective personal brand. You have to be out there. You have to 'Arise and Shine' for your light has come! You have to reflect the glory of God in you.

The second keyword is 'largely uniform perception'. This means that what they know you as in the United Kingdom is what they know you as in the Central African Republic. When people encounter you in Europe, the same solution you offer is what you offer when you're encountered in the United States. People must have a largely uniform perception of who you are promising the world that you are. I often use the example of Coca-Cola. Coca-Cola is the same all over the world, be it in Africa, Asia, Australia, or Europe. An effective personal brand must provide people a uniform perception everywhere. As a multi-talented individual, this is very important. When building your personal brand, in order to create this largely uniform impression of you, you mustn't be trying to build the brand with all your talents or gifts. You must be building your personal brand using your most dominant gift(s), otherwise you will confuse people. It is also important to realise we're talking about people's perceptions here. People have the right to think whatever they want to think of you based on their experience with you. Make people's experience of you and with you a good one. Ensure your experiences, competencies, achievements, and actions going forward reflect the image you are trying to build. This brings me to something else that is very important, the process of building a personal brand, which is referred to as personal branding.

Personal branding is the intentional and conscious effort to create and influence public perception of you by positioning yourself as an expert or authority in your domain, industry or sphere of influence by elevating your credibility and differentiating yourself from others towards increasing your impact and influence.

This definition is very important and has some keywords I would like to expand on so that you can get it. You see, personal branding is a process. While your personal brand is what people say about you, personal branding is what you tell people that you are. An effective personal brand is one that has closed the gap between the two.

The first keyword in that definition is *intentional effort*. It is impossible to build a personal brand without being intentional. It won't work. If you do things anyhow without intentionally questioning whether your actions are in alignment with the image you are trying to build, then you won't be able to build effectively. Personal branding requires your effort to be directed intentionally towards who you are saying to the world that you are, and the solution you bring to the table.

The second keyword is influencing public perception. This is very key because it is not easy to influence people's perception of you. I often say that everyone has a personal brand, the only question is, is it the brand they are intentionally building? Yes, people already have a perception of you before you even think of building a personal brand. Your actions and experiences before now have built a certain degree of perception in the mind of people about you. Now, as you try to rebuild, you have to be intentional not to keep building the former image in the mind of people. When I started to build my brand as The Purpose

Preacher, I had to be intentional. People used to know me as a comedian, Master of Ceremonies, compere, etc. but I wanted to change that because those other brands were conflicting with the new image of the preacher and speaker that I was trying to build. Intentionally, I stopped accepting invitations to compere events or perform jokes for people, no matter how much they wanted to pay me. I must admit, this was not easy, especially when people tempt you with money, but I had to say no so I could influence public perception towards my new brand – The Purpose Preacher. One thing you must know is that repetition breeds retention. The more you repeat what you want people to hold in their minds about you, the more they retain it. But if you keep changing and fidgeting with it because of the lure of money and public praise, you will never be able to build an effective personal brand.

> *Personal branding requires your effort to be directed intentionally towards who you are saying to the world that you are, and the solution you bring to the table*

Another keyword is *'positioning yourself as an authority'*. You have to position yourself as the solution to the problem you are promising the world you solve. This positioning also requires intentionality but most importantly, showing up! You must show up as the solution. You must become the solution, and this takes time. Even though you have the gift, you must look the part. You must now intentionally begin to walk and talk like the brand you are trying to build. The process of becoming takes time and it's a process so you must persevere and be consistent through the process. It may look like your other gifts are wasting away but no, they are not. Positioning would require you to build platforms for yourself to consistently showcase your gifts such that when people mention your name, they mention the problem you solve and vice versa. To be an authority on anything requires that you develop mastery in that thing. The dictionary defines mastery as 'possession or display of great skill or technique'[17]. You must be great at what you do, and to do that requires that you pour your whole life into it. One of the worst things that can happen to anyone is to be average in what they're gifted to do. Yes, it is possible to be average in your gifts. You cannot build a brand being average or mediocre. You have to demonstrate mastery. You have to get results consistently and be able to demonstrate your ability to get results all the time. You must be a student of that niche. You must learn your way to becoming that image you want the world to see you as. The goal is that people begin to point to you as the solution to their problems. They will even point you to their friends.

These days, many people book my coaching services without even reaching out to me first because someone somewhere told them about me. Interestingly, some of the people who told them about me have not even undergone my coaching before, but I have managed to build my brand enough for people to trust that I am an authority! I mentioned being a student of that niche earlier, and I mean it. For instance, I have read over 40 books on purpose and I'm still reading. I'm also writing books on it. I am communicating to the world the promise that if you have any problems with not knowing your purpose or in search of clarity, then you need to find me. I am doing this by consistently showing up every day with the same message. Also, I have demonstrated results in my life and with the lives of others too, so people can trust my brand. This is why they

---

17   https://www.merriam-webster.com/dictionary/mastery

can recommend it to their friends and families all over the world. This is very important if you are trying to build your personal brand too.

Another keyword I would like to talk about is *differentiating yourself from others*. You cannot build an effective personal brand without the element of uniqueness. What makes you different? What makes you unique? What is your unique selling point? In fact, this is a principle when it comes to personal brand. You cannot afford to do things like everyone else. You have to find a way to separate yourself from the pack. And it is not that hard, you just need to embrace that unique attribute about you or adopt something unique that you can be identified with. Some people adopt a colour and they ensure everything about them and their message reflects those colours, from their logos to their designs, to their websites, you see the colours everywhere. For instance, I love the colours yellow and blue and you will see them in my logo and most of the things I do. For others, it's their story. Your story is a unique selling point, trust me. No one has your story. Even though your story may look similar, there are still elements of that story that are unique to you. Les Brown, a world-renowned motivational speaker, tells his story with such gusto that even if you have heard it before you won't even feel it. He tells it with such confidence and art that it sounds new every time because he's learnt to own his uniqueness and that differentiates him from other motivational speakers. For some people, it's their dressing. Whatever is yours, be intentional about it. Celebrate your uniqueness, embrace it and be consistent with it. For me, in my speaking, it's the energy I bring to my game. Every time I speak, I speak with so much passion and energy. I have tried sounding like some of the great speakers I know, trying to be calm and gentle, but I realised it wasn't working for me, so I have learnt to celebrate and embrace my uniqueness. It has now become part of my brand. You will hear people say, *'Dr Samuel will burst the place open'*, or *'Dr Samuel is always on fire'!*. Can you see that people now attribute that energy to my brand?

You cannot build an effective personal brand without the element of uniqueness

I believe you have been convinced it is important for you to build a personal brand with your dominant gifts. You cannot truly live a life of dominion privately. You have to be out there making disciples of the nations with your gifts. It was not a suggestion that we have to disciple the nations, it's a command![18] If we must learn from Jesus, He did not make disciples privately. Jesus had a brand! The Bible talked about Jesus – 'How God anointed Jesus of Nazareth with the Holy Spirit and power, and how he went around doing good and healing all who were under the power of the devil, because God was with him'[19]. He went about doing good. What good are you going about doing with your gift? That's the question I would leave with you in this chapter.

18 Matthew 28:18-20 NIV
19 Acts 10:38 NIV

Chapter 4:

THE REAL VALUE OF ADOPTING THE SOLUTION:

I have shared the solution to the problem you may have if you are multitalented or multi-gifted. The solution I shared is what has worked for me and a lot of other people I have worked with as a coach, people I have studied in the Bible and our world. There was a time I was listening to the late Dr Myles Munroe share about how in his teenage years, he was a renowned musician in his country, Bahamas. In fact, his fame was starting to spread when God revealed his purpose to him, and since then, he had to abandon his music for the purpose of God, which was to preach the purpose and kingdom of God to nations and to help develop the third world. He did that faithfully till he departed the earth. He mentioned that he could have continued with his music, but the world may never have known him, even if the world did, it would not have been with the same magnitude as we did. He would maybe have been popular with the people of his country, but God had more in store for him. As soon as he focused on his gift of speaking and writing, everything changed! He was able to influence the world more than he would have with his music.

Similarly, if I continued to do comedy, compere events, do music as I used to, trying to use all those gifts for different purposes, my life would have been so ineffective. Yes, at the time, my life was all over the place, like the rocking chair going nowhere but making the motion and squeaking here and there. But when I found my purpose and focused on my most dominant gifts to fulfil that purpose, my life changed! It has been amazing since 2016 when I made that discovery and life has been so fulfilling, meaningful, and impactful. I can count my blessings and I want to share some of them with you so that you can get an understanding of why you must adopt this solution as well. The world must discover what you are carrying. Enough of being busy and not effective. Enough of making the motion and not progress. Enough of being that rocking chair that makes a lot of noise and motion yet going nowhere. The time has come for you to become effective and impactful. The time has come for you to leave your imprint on the world with your gifts. The time has come for you to make disciples of nations and be all that God has called you to be. I know this would come with a lot of sacrifices and it won't be easy, but you can do it. If I can do it, so can you. So, let me share some of those values with you so that you can be inspired to act.

You become effective, not just busy

The worst way to live life is to be busy doing what you were not born or called to do. Your fulfilment is really in doing what you have been called to do. Every time spent doing what you are not born to do is wasting the time you're given for what you're meant to do. God takes time very seriously and He wants us to do the same. He wants us to be effective.

The Merriam Webster dictionary defined 'effective' as 'producing a decided, decisive, or desired effect'[20]. If you are going to be effective, you have to find out what effect has been decided for or desired of you way before you were born. Curating your life based on this desire or decision is what your effectiveness is based on. You cannot use an iPad as a chopping board, no

20   https://www.merriam-webster.com/dictionary/effective

matter how much you think it is okay for you to do it, and expect it to be effective. I first heard the term 'defective success' from Sir Fela Durotoye, one of Africa's most gifted speakers. He defined it as 'being successful in what you were not born to do'. There are so many people in our world living defective life yet are seemingly successful. That is dangerous. Imagine working hard here on earth to be 'successful' only for you to get before your Maker and He says, 'So sorry, you wasted your time on earth doing what I did not ask you to do'. That would suck! The most effective way to live is to do what you were born to do.

When I decided to focus my life and gifts on the purpose of God for my life, my effectiveness rose! I felt a lot more effective. Every day, I woke up with a renewed sense of value. You know it when your life is headed in the right direction. No void, no emptiness, just pure joy knowing that your life counts. I tell you this is how God intends for us to live life. The truth is, I was not the only one feeling it. With time, I noticed the world around me started to notice it too. I started getting invites to quarters that matter. For the first time in my life, I felt so valuable and knew it was real! I was not faking it to make it, I was actually on the right course to destiny. As my effectiveness grew, I realised people started to know what to come to me for.

People know what to come to you for

When people mention my name, they immediately associate my name with my purpose – which is to help people discover their purpose. I cannot count how many times over the last two years that people have referred others to me because they couldn't find their purpose or needed clarity. I remember one of those referred to me who booked a clarity session with me saying she was at a masterclass, and the host of the event, someone I'm not even friends with, referred her to me. She had asked in the Masterclass how to discover her purpose and the host's answer blew my mind. She said to this young lady, 'Go on Instagram, and look up 'Dr Samuel Ekundayo – The Purpose Preacher'. He is all about purpose and he will help you. When she told me this, I was blown away! This lady took that advice, paid $199 without even speaking to me first. She believed she would get answers because she had been referred by someone she trusted, someone who hasn't even booked any of my sessions before but probably only heard me speak or saw some of my posts on Instagram a few times.

When I was younger, in my High School days, I remember there was this mango tree in one of my friends' houses. Whenever we closed from school, we would walk to their house, spend over an hour there on the tree plucking mangoes and eating them right there on the tree. The tree gave us shade and not only that we had its delicious fruits for lunch. In the season of mangoes, that tree was our favourite place to be after school. I noticed something however, the tree never moved from where it was. The tree was never at any point in time worried whether we were going to come. The tree maintained its position, bore its fruit and we always gravitated towards it because we knew we would always find the tree there. Amazing, right? In the same way, when you learn to position yourself rightly, bear the fruits (become the solution) that people are looking for, people will come to look for you. Just as the tree never had to leave its place to look for us to present us with its fruits, you too would never have to run helter-skelter. People will come looking for what you are carrying. The reason why people may not be looking for you now is that you have been all over the place. Be the solution you were created to be, and position yourself rightly, and people will come looking for what you're carrying.

One of the key values of getting your most dominant gift right and building a personal brand on it is that you will attract people with the problem that your purpose solves. To be all over the place, attempting to use all your gifts is to deny being known for the exact solution you are carrying. You will confuse people. I am so glad I no longer confuse people like I used to. I have developed myself as the solution to the problem of a lack of clarity of purpose in our world. I have given a TEDx talk about it. I have spoken over 200 times on the topic. I have written books about it and am still writing. I have developed a network of friends and individuals as a result. Life is headed in the upward and forward direction. Nowadays, conference organisers book me from my website to speak at their conferences on the topic of purpose. In fact, some pastors book me and fly me from New Zealand to their countries and when I get to their churches, they would be telling their congregation they were also seeing me for the first time. Isn't that amazing? That's what happens when you discover your most dominant gifts, focus on them, and build a personal brand around them. People surely know what to come to you for.

Also, today, many people, from all over the world book my coaching sessions, attend my masterclasses, and seminars to discover their purpose or gain clarity. I am undoubtedly a product of grace, but I appreciate God for this wisdom to know what my dominant gifts are and focus on them. You too can be sought-after. You too can be the solution to people's problems.

You grow in influence as people are inspired

One of my favourite definitions of influence is from the Merriam-Webster dictionary, which says, 'The act or power of producing an effect without apparent exertion of force or direct exercise of command'[21]. Influence is not in coercing people to do anything but the capacity to cause transformation in people's lives indirectly. I love how Jesus speaks about influence using the parable of yeast[22]. The scripture says, 'The Kingdom

---

21   https://www.merriam-webster.com/dictionary/influence
22   Matthew 13:33 NLT

of Heaven is like the yeast a woman used in making bread. Even though she put only a little yeast in three measures of flour, it permeated every part of the dough'. Only a little yeast in the flour would permeate every part of it and cause it to swell, literally changing the flour into bread! Without the yeast, the flour won't look like dough. This is what the Kingdom of God is really like. You and I are the Kingdom of God made manifest. We are the yeast in the dough of this world. However, you cannot truly manifest as yeast or be influential if you don't yet recognise what you carry. You cannot have influence trying to do everything or solve every problem. Your influence and relevance are heavily dependent on identifying the problem you were born to solve and pouring your entire life into it.

I remember a time I got a book to speak to a church in a country called Belize. I didn't know anyone in the country. In fact, I have never been to that part of the world before. I had to go Google the country as I had not heard about it before the booking came through. The pastor said, 'Man of God, we've been watching you for some months now, following your messages and we would like to have you be a blessing to us'. I couldn't believe someone from a country I have never heard of in my life has been watching and following me. I was blown away! I could not believe it.

A young man sent me an email the other day and said, for years since encountering the late Dr Myles Munroe, he had been looking for someone who preached the message of purpose as passionately as him. He said the day he found me, his search was over. He has since started following me. He followed me for a whole year and read my books, before sending me that email. This is the power of influence. The capacity to cause a transformation in the lives of others without any exertion of force or coercion. God can do the same with you as well if you would stop trying to use all your gifts at once. Find God's purpose for your life, and build a brand on your most dominant gifts. Your value will be communicated to your world and generations will look for you for what you carry.

One of the terms I have come to fall in love with recently is 'Trans-generational Influence'. I define it as influence beyond your lifespan. I am convinced that when the Bible says 'God has put eternity in our hearts'[23], it was not a mistake. God was intentional about it. He wanted us to have a desire to live beyond our lifetime. Fortunately, that was not God just wishfully thinking. He built that desire and possibility inside of us. The source of your trans-generational influence is in the purpose of God for your life. It is rooted in pouring your entire life into solving the problem you were born to solve – being known for and as the solution to that problem. Your life will not only affect your generation but for generations after you. The Bible is full of heroes and heroines whose influence transcends generations. I mean, Jesus Christ is a key example. I am often amazed at how one man would live for just 33.5 years, yet the world can't forget Him. He lives through the pages of every historical revelation and record. All the ancient books of this world have Jesus in them. Some misconstrued His mission and identity but they still had him! WOW! What a life!

QUOTE: The source of your trans-generational influence is in the purpose of God for your life.

I could almost hear you say but Jesus is God, so that's expected. How about ordinary men like Moses who was not perfect and even towards the end of his life had his weakness get the better of him, yet still lives on in our hearts, books, and lips, thousands of years after? What about a prostitute like Rahab, who was not even a Jew but believed in the God of the Jews and as a result, did something noble – saving the spies in the land of Jericho, and today we can't stop talking about her heroics? How about

---

23 Ecclesiastes 3:11

that woman who saved up her wages to get the alabaster jar of perfume, broke it, and poured it on Jesus, anointed him with it. The people present couldn't understand what she was doing. It didn't make sense how she would pour her entire wages on Jesus! But Jesus made a statement we must all study. He said, '*Truly I tell you, wherever this gospel is preached throughout the world, what she has done will also be told, in memory of her*'.[24] What a pronunciation. Indeed, we are still talking about that woman.

One of the most effective ways to live life is to be driven by eternity. Many people waste their lifetime focusing on visible and temporary things but that is not how God intends for us to live. He wants our minds to be on invisible and eternal things. There is only one way to help our mind be on invisible and eternal things, it is when we live for the purpose of God for our lives and not our earthly mundane desires. Paul was clear in his advice to us, 'Set *your* minds on the things above, not the things on the earth'[25]. It is only when we're driven by eternity that our influence can last beyond our lifetime. People who are driven by eternity live differently, they talk differently, they move differently, they do things differently. They are not seduced by the rat race or the lure of position and title. Their purpose is their watchword and the commendation of the Father is their reward. You must completely seek to be a person of influence not a person of titles. You must seek to lead in your calling. You must be a steward of your gifts to your generation and the ones to come. When God created man, He blessed us and asked us to be fruitful and multiply, He had influence in mind because to multiply means 'to end up with more than you started out with'. God wants you to end up with more than He gave you. For this to happen, you have to effectively steward what He has given you. You have to use it correctly. You have to use it well.

---

24   Matthew 26:13 NIV
25   Colossians 3:2 BLB

I am reminded of Matthew 25:29, where Jesus said, 'To those who use well what they are given, even more will be given, and they will have an abundance. But from those who do nothing, even what little they have will be taken away'. When I read that scripture, it was clear there are three ways to use what God has given us. We can either use it well, use it poorly, or not use it at all. In this book, I have shared with you a key to help you use your gifts well. If you follow the solution in this book, you will tend towards abundance – a life of influence beyond your lifetime and generation. That is my mission. I am on a mission to influence generations beyond my lifetime. I am on a mission to touch the lives of generations yet unborn. I am on a mission to live fully and die empty! Are you with me?

One of the most effective ways to live life is to be driven by eternity.

You in turn increase in value.

The Merriam-Webster dictionary defines value as 'the monetary worth (market price) of something'. It is important to talk about this definition of value because I can imagine someone asking, 'Will this solution put food on the table for me? I mean, isn't it more logical to use all your gifts at once and hope that at least one of them will bring you value or reward you monetarily'? On the contrary, you cannot become valuable by being common! You only become valuable by being unique and rare!

Why do we value petrol so much? We pay a premium to put fuel in our tanks because we cannot commonly find fuel anywhere. It's a rare commodity. So is gold. We pay a premium for gold because it is rare! Valuable things in life are very rare. Both examples of gold and petrol come from digging the ground, and not just any ground but rare places to find these precious

things. To make yourself rare is to recognise your most dominant gift and choose to focus your life on it to serve the world.
But when you're a commoner, no one will see you as a person
of value.

One thing about valuable people is that they command their worth. You determine how much you would be paid.

One thing about valuable people is that they command their
worth. You determine how much you would be paid. People
don't tell you how much you would earn, you determine the
price they would pay. This is my story to the glory of God. The
world does not determine my economy. My job does not determine my economy. I determine my economy. The more valuable I become, the more people seek me. The more they seek
for me, the more demand they place on my time, as a result, my
time is valuable. The more valuable my time is worth, the more
I increase the price to have access to me. Everything I have
shared with you in the pages of this book is the story of my life.
They are principles I live by and have in turn changed my life.
You too can give them a go and watch your life take a new turn!

Chapter 5

YOUR DELIVERANCE FROM THE RAT RACE

The Oxford Dictionary defines the rat race as 'A way of life in which people are caught up in a fiercely competitive struggle for wealth or power'. Too many people are living every single day in survival mode. They are driven by competition to become somebody in life. The truth is, you were already made somebody. God did not create anyone useless or a nobody. In God's grand scheme of things, we're all a success. God created us to thrive, not to survive. When God created us, He blessed us and told us to have dominion. He was making a demand on the abilities He has given us to become all that He has created us to be.

Please don't let the rat race be your drive. Avoid the seduction of the rat race by all means possible. If you practice the principle I have shared with you in this book, I can promise you that you will not live your life for survival. You will surely dominate in the territory that God has given you. You will demonstrate the authority that comes with it. The Greek word for 'authority' in the Bible is *'exousia'* which means 'delegated influence'. God delegated His influence on us here on earth and when we recognise His purpose in our lives and our most dominant gift, we enter into the realm of authority in which God's influence is displayed in our lives. We become the kings of our domain and begin to extend God's kingdom in that realm – whether it is business, education, arts, entertainment, or media. God does not want you to live a mediocre life. He wants you to live like a king here on earth, of course, not ruling over people but reigning in the domain of influence He has given you.

You cannot reign if you are ineffective or do not know your domain. You cannot reign trying to be in several domains at the same time. You cannot reign being covetous of another person's domain. Find yours, stay there, and pour your entire life into it. This is your key to living above the rat race. This is your key to avoiding the life of fierce competition for earthly luxury. That mentality can imprison you for life because it's a bottomless pit. The desire to acquire is often endless in the rat race, which is why it must not be your pre-occupation. But when purpose and eternity are your drive and motivation, earthly things do not become do or die for you. They do not become the basis for what you do. What they would be are by-products or rewards for what you're sent to do. Just like that scripture tells us, 'But seek first his kingdom and his righteousness, **and all these things will be given to you as well.**' God wants to give us wealth, riches, and money but He does not want us to make them our pursuit. He wants our ultimate pursuit to be the kingdom of God and His righteousness. He will then make sure we lack nothing! Provision is a key part of God's plans for our lives. God has not called anyone to impoverish them.

I was taking a workshop a while back and a lady in the audience asked me a question. She said, 'I know the purpose of God for my life but I can't follow it now because it cannot pay the bills. I don't want to become poor'. While I understand the genuineness of her question, I couldn't help but see through her ignorance.

Provision is a key part of God's plans for our lives. God has not called anyone to impoverish them.

Are you one of those people who believe that following the purpose of God will impoverish you? I mean, you feel if you abandon everything and follow Him, God is not faithful enough to showcase His glory in your life. Trust me, this is a question on the lips of many people. I used to have this question too until I made a discovery that changed my life. Peter asked Jesus a very important question. He said, 'Excuse me, sir, "we have given up everything to follow you, what are we going to get?' The answer Jesus gave is worth studying. He said, 'There is no man that hath left house, or brethren, or sisters, or father, or mother, or wife, or children, or lands, for my sake, and the gospel's, But he shall receive a hundredfold now in this time, houses, and brethren, and sisters, and mothers, and children, and lands, with persecutions; and in the world to come eternal life'[26] God promises that if you pursue His kingdom, you will be both earthly and eternally rewarded.

No one follows God to become wretched and hungry. Provision follows every vision God has given you. While you will suffer persecution in His name for abandoning everything to follow Him because the world would not understand, rest assured that God is faithful. He will never leave you or forsake you. God wants to give you all that pertains to life and godliness, but He requires that you follow Him fully, and wholeheartedly, without doubting His faithfulness in your life.

---

26   Mark 10:29-30

So what will happen to my other gifts?

I know you have this question on your mind. God does not waste resources, so He gave you those gifts to help you fulfil His purpose for your life as well without a doubt. But you cannot start out trying to use all the gifts at the same time. That will make you ineffective. However, as you are known for that one thing, and your brand has been tested and trusted, you can now begin to bring your other gifts to work, and rest assuredly, it won't affect your effectiveness.

In my life, you would be amazed at how many of my gifts are brought into helping people discover their purpose. Now, before some of my ministrations, I play the keyboard, raise some worship songs to open the heavens, and sometimes also close my messages with these. What I have noticed is that God uses my worship to open the heavens such that by the time I speak, God is already at work in the hearts and minds of those listening to me. So amazing! My ability to do graphics and develop websites now helps in creating content for my brand. I design some of my flyers myself and I have done that for years. I developed my website – samuelekundayo.com – myself. I have also developed various websites under my brand. While right now, I have some people who now work for me and serve with me in these areas, when I started these gifts/skills were very useful in fulfilling my purpose when I could not afford to pay people to do them for me.

Apart from that, in my coaching, I have seen some of my technical knowledge and know-how become so useful to my clients. My ability to understand software development and the intricacies surrounding it has become such massive value to helping other people build their brands. For some, I have created training programmes that have helped my clients, masterclasses to help them see the value in some of these skills and use them to grow their brands. I stand out as a coach because these gifts and skills are all channelled to helping people discover God's purpose for their lives and maximising their potentials towards a fulfilled, impactful and influential life. God can use all your gifts this way too but you can't afford to become the jack of all trade, master of none, it will lead to ineffectiveness and oftentimes, frustration.

Enough about me. I have also seen this at work in the lives of some great people I know. A typical example I know is Bishop T.D. Jakes. Very few people know He has a company that produces music and films. Besides the fact that He is a renowned preacher and author, he is into films and music. I want to believe he's had a passion for these things before he became known, but he was not known for those things because they were not his dominant gifts. His speaking and preaching were the most dominant. His message 'Woman thou art loosed' appears to be the message that brought him to the limelight after several years of preaching. Following His success on the pulpit, he has gone on to use his influence to impact the world through films, TV shows, books, and music.

It is easy to look at Bishop T.D. Jakes now and wants to begin where he is now. That would be misleading if you don't know his story. Not everyone who is known for something today began with everything they could do. They started with their most dominant gift first, and they grew a tested and trusted brand, then they are easily able to diversify without it affecting all they've built and worked for. You too can learn from them. While it is surely a blessing to be multi-gifted by God, we must learn the wisdom to help us effectively maximise those gifts to fulfil the purpose of God and to extend His kingdom on earth.

It is very germane to also realise that God gave us those gifts because He knows we can maximise them. The Bible, in the parable of the talents, relays to us that God gives us gifts in the proportion that abilities can carry – 'And unto one he gave five talents, to another two, and to another one, to every man according to his several abilities...'[27] The number of gifts you have is directly proportional to your ability. God knows you can maximise those gifts that is why He gave them to you. Your ability is not the question. Your effectiveness is the question, and that is what this book helps with.

> *The number of gifts you have is directly proportional to your ability. God knows you can maximise those gifts that is why He gave them to you.*

It is my prayer for you that you imbibe the principles and solutions in this book to help you maximise your talents for effective use and the extension of God's kingdom. If this book has been a blessing to you, I would love to hear from you. You will find my email address at the back of the book. Send me an email sometime. God bless you, keep you, and cause His face to shine on you in Jesus' name. Amen!

I believe in you.

---

27   Matthew 25:15 KJV

www.ingramcontent.com/pod-product-compliance
Lightning Source LLC
Chambersburg PA
CBHW071232130726
47998CB00003B/924